SCHOLASTIC

writing guides

With interactive resources on CD-ROM

Realistic Stories

for ages
9–11

Alison Kelly
and
Jillian Powell

Terms and conditions

IMPORTANT – PERMITTED USE AND WARNINGS – READ CAREFULLY BEFORE USING

Credits

Authors
Alison Kelly and
Jillian Powell

Development Editors
Rachel Mackinnon and
Marion Archer

Assistant Editor
Alex Albrighton

Series Designer
Anna Oliwa

Designers
Paul Stockmans and
Liz Gilbert

Cover Illustration
Mark Oliver

Illustrations
Andy Keylock

CD-ROM Development
CD-ROM developed in
association with Infuze Ltd

Mixed Sources
Product group from well-managed
forests and other controlled sources
www.fsc.org Cert no. TT-COC-002769
© 1996 Forest Stewardship Council
FSC

Text © 2010, Jillian Powell
Text © 2002, 2010 Alison Kelly
© 2010 Scholastic Ltd

Designed using Adobe InDesign

Published by Scholastic Ltd,
Book End
Range Road
Witney
Oxfordshire
OX29 0YD
www.scholastic.co.uk

Printed by Bell & Bain
1 2 3 4 5 6 7 8 9   0 1 2 3 4 5 6 7 8 9

British Library Cataloguing-in-Publication Data
A catalogue record for this book is available from the British Library.
ISBN 978-1407-11264-0

The right of Alison Kelly and Jillian Powell to be identified as the authors of this work has been asserted by them in accordance with the Copyright, Designs and Patents Act 1988.

Extracts from the Primary National Strategy's Primary Framework for Literacy (2006) www.standards.dfes.gov.uk/primaryframework © Crown copyright. Reproduced under the terms of the Click Use Licence.

Acknowledgments
The publishers gratefully acknowledge permission to reproduce the following copyright material: **David Highman Associates** for the use of two illustrations by Nick Sharratt from *The Suitcase Kid* by Jacqueline Wilson, illustrations © 1992, Nick Sharratt (1992, Doubleday) and for the electronic use of an extract from *The Suitcase Kid* by Jacqueline Wilson © 1992 Jacqueline Wilson (1992, Doubleday). **Scholastic Children's Books** for the use of an extract from *The Battle of Bubble and Squeak* by Philippa Pearce © 1978, Philippa Pearce (1978, Andre Deutsche). **Random House Group Ltd** for the print use of an extract for *The Suitcase Kid* by Jacqueline Wilson © 1992, Jacqueline Wilson (1992, Doubleday).
Every effort has been made to trace copyright holders for the works reproduced in this book, and the publishers apologise for any inadvertent omissions.

CD-ROM Minimum specifications:

Windows 2000/XP/Vista		Mac OSX 10.4
Processor: 1 GHz	RAM: 512 MB	Graphics card: 32bit
Audio card: Yes	CD-ROM drive speed: 8x	Hard disk space: 200MB
Screen resolution: 800x600		

Contents

Introduction: Realistic Stories

The *Writing Guides* series aims to inspire and motivate children as writers by using creative approaches. Each *Writing Guide* contains activities and photocopiable resources designed to develop children's understanding of a particular genre (for example, fairy stories). The activities are in line with the requirements of the National Curriculum and the recommendations in the *Primary Framework for Literacy*. The teacher resource books are accompanied by a CD-ROM containing a range of interactive activities and resources.

What's in the book?

The *Writing Guides* series provides a structured approach to developing children's writing. Each book is divided into four sections.

Section 1: **Using good examples**
Three text extracts are provided to explore the typical features of the genre.

Section 2: **Developing writing**
There are ten short, focussed writing tasks in this section. These are designed to develop children's ability to use the key features of the genre in their own writing. The teachers' notes explain the objective of each activity and provide guidance on delivery, including how to use the photocopiable pages and the materials on the CD-ROM.

Section 3: **Writing**
The three writing projects in this section require the children to produce an extended piece of writing using the key features of the genre.

Section 4: **Review**
This section consists of a 'Self review', 'Peer review' and 'Teacher review'. These can be used to evaluate how effectively the children have met the writing criteria for the genre.

What's on the CD-ROM?

The accompanying CD-ROM contains a range of motivating activities and resources. The activities can be used for independent work or can be used on an interactive whiteboard to enhance group teaching.
Each CD-ROM contains:
- three text extracts that illustrate the typical features of the genre
- interactive versions of selected photocopiable pages
- four photographs and an audio file to create imaginative contexts for writing
- a selection of writing templates and images which can be used to produce extended pieces of writing.

The interactive activities on the CD-ROM promote active learning and support a range of teaching approaches and learning styles. For example, drag and drop and sequencing activities will support kinaesthetic learners.

Talk for writing

Each *Writing Guide* uses the principles of 'Talk for writing' to support children's writing development by providing opportunities for them to rehearse ideas orally in preparation for writing. 'Talk for writing' is promoted using a variety of teaching strategies including discussions, questioning and drama activities (such as, developing imaginative dialogue – see *Fantasy Stories for Ages 9–11*).

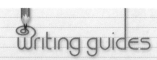

How to use the CD-ROM

Start screen: click on the 'Start' button to go to the main menu.

This section contains brief instructions on how to use the CD-ROM. For more detailed guidance, go to 'How to use the CD-ROM' on the start screen or click on the 'Help' button located in the top right-hand corner of the screen.

Installing the CD-ROM

Follow the instructions on the disk to install the CD-ROM onto your computer. Once the CD-ROM is installed, navigate to the program location and double click on the program icon to open it.

Main menu screen

Main menu

The main menu provides links to all of the writing activities and resources on the CD-ROM. Clicking on a button from the main menu will take you to a sub-menu that lists all of the activities and resources in that section. From here you have the option to 'Launch' the interactive activities, which may contain more than one screen, or print out the activities for pupils to complete by hand.

If you wish to return to a previous menu, click the 'Menu' button in the top right-hand corner of the screen; this acts as a 'back' button.

Screen tools

A range of simple writing tools that can be used in all of the writing activities are contained in the toolbar at the bottom of the screen.

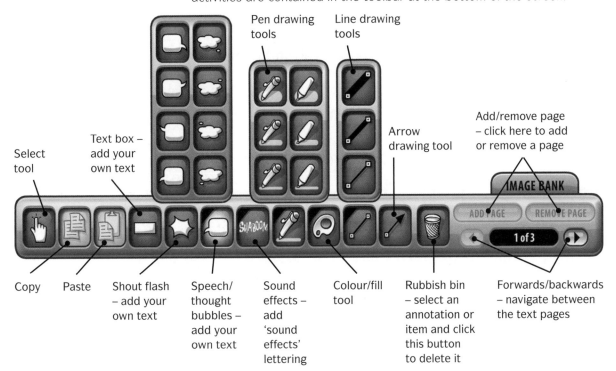

Select tool

Text box – add your own text

Pen drawing tools

Line drawing tools

Arrow drawing tool

Add/remove page – click here to add or remove a page

Copy

Paste

Shout flash – add your own text

Speech/thought bubbles – add your own text

Sound effects – add 'sound effects' lettering

Colour/fill tool

Rubbish bin – select an annotation or item and click this button to delete it

Forwards/backwards – navigate between the text pages

Print

Save your work to chosen files

Open – navigate to your saved file to open your previous work

Reset the page

Printing and saving work

All of the resources on the CD-ROM are printable. You can also save and retrieve any annotations made on the writing activities. Click on the 'Controls' tab on the right-hand side of the screen to access the 'Print', 'Open', 'Save' and 'Reset screen' buttons.

View all thumbnails by clicking on the arrows

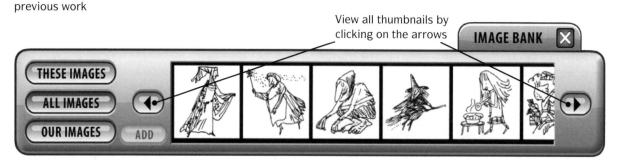

Image bank – click and drag an image to add it to an activity

Image bank

Each CD-ROM has an 'Image bank' containing images appropriate to the genre being taught. Click on the tab at the bottom right of the screen to open the 'Image bank'. On the left-hand side there are three large buttons.

- The 'These images' button will display only the images associated with the specific activity currently open.
- The 'All images' button will display all the photographs and illustrations available on the CD-ROM.
- The 'Our images' button will contain any images you or the children have added to the CD-ROM.

Press the left or right arrows to scroll through the images available. Select an image and drag and drop it into the desired location on the screen. If necessary, resize the image using the arrow icon that appears at the bottom right of the image.

You can upload images to the 'Image bank', including digital photographs or images drawn and scanned into the computer. Click on 'Our images' and then 'Add' to navigate to where the image is stored. A thumbnail picture will be added to the gallery.

Writing your own story

Each CD-ROM contains a selection of blank writing templates. The fiction genre templates will be categorised under the button 'My story' and the non-fiction templates will be categorised under 'My recount' or 'My writing'. The writing templates encourage the children to produce an extended piece of genre writing. They can also add images, speech bubbles and use other tools to enhance their work.

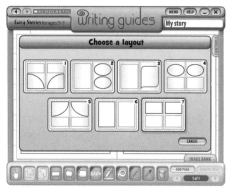

The fiction titles also include a cover template for the children to use. They can customise their cover by adding their own title, blurb and images.

Section 1
Using good examples

Realistic stories

Realistic stories are a relatively new genre in children's literature, popularised by authors such as Jacqueline Wilson and Anne Fine. They have familiar, everyday settings and plots centred on real issues or dilemmas that children may themselves be experiencing such as family break up, bereavement, moving house and bullying. Events typically revolve around characters within family, friendship or community groups. The story may be told by a first-person narrator or in the third person, but usually they focus on a character who is grappling with the issue, sometimes alone and facing opposition from or conflict with others. Relationships are important and often the central character grows or learns from experience during the story.

Through shared reading of a range of realistic stories and the extracts in this section, children will become familiar with the key conventions of the genre and be able to draw on them for their own writing. The most fruitful writing in this genre is likely to come from personal experience, so you may like to suggest that children use this as a starting point for ideas. Keeping a diary or journal is a useful way for them to collect experiences and ideas that they can use in their narrative writing.

The children will also develop their understanding of the genre by reading a wide range of titles. A useful starting point is other stories by the authors featured – for example, *The Story of Tracy Beaker* or *The Bed and Breakfast Star* by Jacqueline Wilson; *The Way to Sattin Shore* and short story collections by Philippa Pearce. They can also explore titles by other authors such as Dick King-Smith's *The Crowstarver* (mental handicap) and *The Eighteenth Emergency* by Betsy Byars (bullying).

Links to the Primary Framework

Developing understanding of and having opportunities to write narrative texts is an important part of literacy development. The Primary Framework for Literacy provides detailed guidance for teaching and learning about realistic stories at Key Stage 2 (Year 3 Narrative Unit 1 'Stories with familiar settings'; Year 4 Narrative Unit 4 'Stories which raise issues/dilemmas'). The genre also falls within the Narrative text type: contemporary fiction and the remit of Year 5 Narrative Unit 1 'Novels and stories by significant children's authors' and Year 6 Narrative Unit 1 'Fiction genres'.

Realistic story features

Plot
- Chronological narrative plot.
- Plot involves problem or issue that must be resolved.
- Problem resolved in a satisfying way at the end.

Language
- First- or third-person narrative.
- Typically past tense, can be present tense.
- Dialogue progresses action and reveals character.

Characters
- Leading character that we empathise with.
- Strong realistic characters.

Setting
- Realistic and familiar.

Extract 1: The Suitcase Kid

What's on the CD-ROM

The Suitcase Kid
- Text extract to read and discuss.

Confidant
- Fill in the speech bubbles to show what the characters might say.

This extract is from a story by Jacqueline Wilson which many children will already be familiar with. The author's work shows how 'issues' can provide the focus and plot for realistic stories and demonstrates a first-person narrative.

- Open the extract from the CD-ROM and read it with the children, going over any difficult vocabulary as necessary. Ask: *What is happening in Andrea's family and why are they seeing the counsellor? What emotions are they feeling?* Write a list of descriptive words with the children – for example, 'angry', 'upset', 'confused', 'sad'.

- Organise the children into pairs. Give each pair a copy of photocopiable page 13 'What's it all about?' to complete. They should scan the text carefully to help them complete the statements.

- Open 'Confidant' from the CD-ROM. Check that the children understand what a confidant is (someone you confide in). Explain to the children that they are going to imagine what each character might say about the meeting with the counsellor to their confidant. Invite them to rehearse orally what each character might say and type the dialogue into the boxes. Alternatively, they can use photocopiable page 14.

Extract 2: The Battle of Bubble and Squeak

What's on the CD-ROM

The Battle of Bubble and Squeak
- Text extract to read and discuss.

Between the lines
- Drag the arrows to match the characters' feelings to the correct evidence.

This extract is from another realistic story the children may already be familiar with. In contrast with Extract 1, it is written as a third-person narrative, with dialogue revealing the feelings of the different characters. The extract shows how an event or incident can trigger a plot line.

- Open the extract from the CD-ROM and read it with the children. Ask: *What is Mrs Sparrow so angry about and what is likely to happen as a consequence?*

- Discuss how the author reveals how characters are feeling, through description ('Tears were streaming down her cheeks') and through dialogue ('Come and see what your – your THINGS have done!').

- Open 'Between the lines' from the CD-ROM. As a shared activity, work through the statements about how the characters are feeling and match the evidence accordingly. Alternatively, the children can complete photocopiable page 15.

- When they have finished, discuss which evidence comes in the form of dialogue and which in the form of description. Encourage the children to explore other passages from the novel or from other realistic novels, looking for more examples of dialogue and description that reveal characters' feelings.

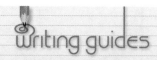

Extract 3: The Locker Room

What's on the CD-ROM

The Locker Room
- Text extract to read, discuss and edit.

Verb match
- Drag and drop the missing verbs to complete the sentences.

This extract invites the children to empathise with the main character Louis, who finds himself the target of a notorious school bully. It shows how choosing words such as strong active verbs, can quicken the pace during dramatic episodes and also demonstrates the use of a page turner or cliffhanger: what will Louis do when Thug steals his homework? On the CD-ROM the text is editable and you can highlight words, phrases and language features.

- Open the extract from the CD-ROM and read it with the children, going over any difficult vocabulary as necessary. Ask them to describe the situation and how Louis is feeling. Elicit the term 'bullying' and discuss the different ways Theo bullies Louis (physically, by blocking his way and almost crushing his fingers, and verbally by making fun of the way he speaks). Consider the setting and the fact that it is scarier because Louis is alone with the bully.

- Open 'Verb match' from the CD-ROM. Invite the children to examine the verbs closely and drag and drop them into the correct spaces. Alternatively, children can complete photocopiable page 16.

- Consider as a shared activity how the strong, active verbs progress the action and also convey Theo's threatening demeanour towards Louis and Louis' feelings of trepidation and anxiety.

Poster: Big issues!

What's on the CD-ROM

Big issues!
- Read and discuss the information on the poster.
- Roll over the text to reveal more information.

The Suitcase Kid, The Battle of Bubble and Squeak, and The Locker Room
- Text extracts to read and discuss.

The poster displays a summary of key features of realistic stories, framed as placards on a campaign or protest march (one of the issues that might trigger a plot for a realistic story).

- The children can study the poster to become familiar with generic features and also refer back to it when writing their own realistic stories or evaluating other examples of the genre.

- Display the poster from the CD-ROM. Roll over the text and work through the tips as they appear.

- Hand out copies of photocopiable page 18 'Big issues!' and explain to the children that they can refer back to this poster when they need to check their own realistic stories or assess other examples of the genre.

- When the children are familiar with the poster, hand out photocopiable page 17 'Cross check' and talk through the list. Ask the children to work in pairs to complete the photocopiable sheet, referring back to all three text extracts.

- Encourage the children to collect stories or ideas from local newspapers, magazines or message boards that could provide the stimulus for a realistic story – for example, the story of a local school closing down or a protest against a new road being built.

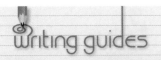

Extract 1: The Suitcase Kid

When my parents split up they didn't know what to do with me. My mum wanted me to go and live with her. My dad wanted me to go and live with him. I didn't want to go and live at my mum's new place or my dad's new place. I wanted to stay living in our *old* place, Mulberry Cottage, the three of us together. Four, counting my pet Sylvanian family spotted rabbit Radish.

There were all these arguments about who would get custody of me. I thought they were talking about custard at first. I hate custard because you can never tell when there's going to be a lump and it sticks in your throat and makes you shudder.

My mum got mad and my dad got mad and I got mad too. I felt *I* was being split up. Half of me wanted to side with Mum. Half of me wanted to side with Dad. It was much easier for Radish. She just sided with me. She lives in my pocket so there's never been any hassle over who gets custody of her.

We had to go for family counselling…

But this lady saw me fiddling about in my pocket and she got a glimpse of Radish. I like to hold her tight when I'm feeling funny.

'Oh, what a dear little toy. Do let me have a look,' she said, in that silly voice grown-ups always use when they're trying to get you to like them…

You'd have thought I was two years old, not ten. I just shrugged and shook my head.

'That's Radish,' said Mum. 'Andrea's had her for years and years. She's a very important member of our family.'

'Actually, I bought Radish for Andrea. As a silly Saturday present. I like to give her a little treat every now and then,' said Dad.

'You did not give Andrea Radish! *I* bought her one Christmas to go in Andrea's stocking,' said Mum.

'Look, I can vividly remember buying that rabbit in the corner shop–'

'They don't even sell Sylvanian families at the corner shop. I bought it from the toy shop in town and–'

I snatched Radish back and put my hand gently over her ears. She can't stand to hear them arguing.

from *The Suitcase Kid* by Jacqueline Wilson.

Text © 1992, Jacqueline Wilson.

Extract 2: The Battle of Bubble and Squeak

In his school trousers and his pyjama top, Sid flew downstairs. His mother met him at the bottom of the stairs. Tears were streaming down her cheeks; she also looked unspeakably angry. "Come and see what your – your THINGS have done!"

She dragged him into the living room. The room was still in semi-darkness because the curtains had not yet been drawn back. But the gloom was shot by strong beams of light coming through two large ragged holes in the curtains. The holes were just behind the cage, and by the light through them Sid could see that the inside of the gerbil cage was littered with scraps and crumbs of scarlet. One gerbil, sitting up watchfully, seemed to be wiping its mouth free of a scarlet thread.

"They've eaten my best curtains," said Mrs Sparrow.

Peggy had followed Sid, and now Amy and Bill Sparrow were crowding to see, Amy holding tight to Bill.

Amy peeped and peered. "I didn't know gerbils ate curtains."

"They don't *eat* them," said Peggy. "They just gnaw at them."

"They've ruined them," said Mrs Sparrow.

"Can't you mend them?" asked Bill Sparrow.

"Can't *I* mend them!"

"I'll mend them," said Sid. "I'll draw the edges of the holes together. I saw you mending that tear in my duffle coat, when it had caught on the barbed wire. I'll buy red cotton exactly to match, and I'll mend it. Peggy'll help me, won't you, Peg?"

"Yes," said Peggy; "but – but –"

"But you can't," said their mother. "Your duffle coat was just torn: there was nothing missing. These curtains have been *gnawed away*. Big bits are missing, all chewed up at the bottom of those wretched creatures' cage."

"I'll do something, Mum!" cried Sid. "I could buy some more of the red stuff to patch the holes with. I've pocket money saved up. I could buy you new curtains. Mum, I tell you what –"

"No," said his mother, "I'm not thinking of the curtains now."

"But Mum, listen –"

"No," said his mother, "no, no, NO! Not another day in this house if I can help it! They go!"

'But, Mum –"

"THEY GO!"

from *The Battle of Bubble and Squeak* by Philippa Pearce.

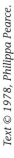

Section 1: Using good examples

Extract 3: The Locker Room

Thug was standing across the doorway of the locker room. His real name was Theo but everyone called him Thug and it was easy to see why.

"Excuse me," Louis said.

Thug stood his ground.

"I need to get to my locker."

Thug glared at him. He moved a bit, just enough for Louis to get through, but not without having to push him. Louis felt his heart quicken.

He marched quickly over to his locker and pulled out his school bag.

Bang! Thug punched the door shut. Only the strap of Louis' bag, which had got caught in the door frame, stopped his fingers from being crushed.

"Hey, you nearly…" his words tailed off. He was alone in the locker room with Thug and it seemed like Thug had got it in for him.

"You got a problem?" Thug asked him.

"No…I…I'm just in a bit of a hurry," Louis stammered.

"What you got in there?" Thug asked, eyeing Louis' bag.

"Nothing. A banana I think. You can have it if you want," Louis said, aware how pathetic that sounded.

"Banana?" Thug began to make monkey noises. "What do you think I am, a chimp or something?"

"I just meant, that's all there is in the bag," Louis said, trying to sound calm. "A banana and my prep."

"Prep?"

Louis had never heard a word said with so much contempt.

"Prep? Your prep?" Thug repeated.

"I mean homework. That's what we used to call it at my old school."

"Oh." Now Thug was putting on an absurd posh voice. "That's what we used to call it at our old school is it? Well get used to it, you're not at that snobby school now. It's homework here. And since you've done it and I haven't, I'll be needing that."

In a flash, Thug grabbed Louis' bag and snatched out his homework. He let the bag drop, the banana flying out like a boomerang.

"Thanks ever so," he hissed in the same scathing voice.

What's it all about?

● Read the text carefully then complete the statements below.

1. Andrea's family had to leave Mulberry Cottage because _____

_____

2. The family is seeing a counsellor because _____

_____

3. Andrea gets the words _____ and _____ muddled up.

4. Andrea is upset because _____

_____

5. Mum and Dad argue about _____

_____

6. Andrea likes to keep Radish in her pocket because _____

_____

7. When the counsellor talks to Andrea _____

_____

8. The reason Andrea covers Radish's ears is _____

_____

Confidant

● After the meeting with the counsellor, what might each character say to their confidant?

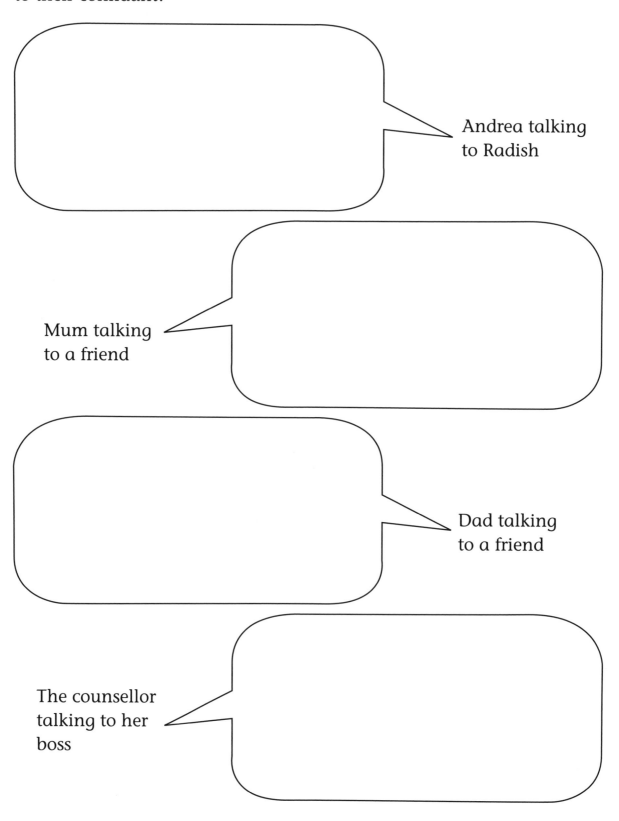

Andrea talking to Radish

Mum talking to a friend

Dad talking to a friend

The counsellor talking to her boss

Between the lines

● Read the extract. Write down some evidence from the text that shows the following.

Sid is in a panic.

Mum is feeling angry.

The curtains are really important to Mum.

Mum hates the gerbils.

Mum blames Sid.

Mr Sparrow is trying to calm things down.

Sid will do anything to keep the gerbils.

Mum has made her mind up.

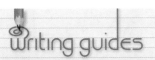

Section 1: Using good examples

Verb match

● Choose appropriate verbs from the list below to fit the spaces.

Thug _____ at Louis.

Thug _____ his ground.

Thug _____ the door shut.

Louis _____ quickly over to his locker.

"I'm just in a bit of a hurry," Louis _____.

He _____ Louis' bag and _____ out his homework.

"Thanks ever so," he _____ in the same scathing voice.

snatched	stammered	glared	hissed
punched	marched	grabbed	stood

● Choose three verbs and suggest a word or phrase that could replace them.

1._____

2._____

3._____

● Pick a verb that tells us something about each character and explain how.

Character	Verb	What it tells us
Theo		
Louis		

Cross check

- Read all three extracts then answer the questions for each below.

	Extract 1	Extract 2	Extract 3
Who are the main characters?			
What is the setting?			
What is the issue or topic?			
What makes us want to read on?			
Choose one character and describe how they are feeling.			
Write down some evidence from the text that reveals their feelings.			

Big issues!

Opening hook leads reader into the story.

Scenario or issue to trigger a plot line.

First-person or third-person narrative.

Familiar settings.

Realistic characters.

Dialogue progresses plot and reveals characters' feelings.

A problem or dilemma to resolve.

Problem resolved in a satisfying way.

Illustrations © 2010, Andy Keylock/Beehive Illustration.

Section 2
Developing writing

Developing realistic story writing
The activities in this section provide opportunities for children to explore the key elements of the genre in terms of plot, character and setting. They guide children through the process of thinking up scenarios or issues and considering settings, all of which can trigger ideas for plots. The children will identify and experiment with three types of writing which they will use in realistic stories: description, dialogue and action. They will also think about narrative stance and whether a first- or third-person narrator will work best for their plots. The activities provide scaffolded support for developing plot structure, fleshing out main characters, crafting dialogue and describing realistic settings. They also focus on style and generate vocabulary for realistic stories.

- Plot: The children have opportunities to map out plots for realistic stories in order to identify generic features and experiment with different pathways for developing a plot line.

- Setting: The children are given opportunities to think how settings can trigger events in a plot and also produce dilemmas or issues for their characters to face.

- Character: The children focus on developing key characters through description and dialogue, using drama and role play to improvise and develop dialogue.

How to use the activities
Each activity is accompanied by detailed teachers' notes giving guidance on delivery, including how to use the photocopiable sheets at the end of the section and the materials on the CD-ROM. The children are encouraged to experiment with a variety of forms. There is strong emphasis on pair or group discussion and role play throughout this section. This will help children get to the heart of issues they are exploring and to empathise with their characters, as well as developing speaking and listening skills. The activities can be adapted to suit different class situations. They should be modelled for the whole class or smaller groups using the whiteboard, before children are asked to undertake independent work.

Activity breakdown

Plot
- Thinking about issues (page 20)
- Trigger points (page 20)
- Storyboard (page 21)
- Campaigns and conflicts (page 22)

Setting
- Subjects and scenarios (page 21)
- Scene change (page 22)

Character
- The lead role (page 23)
- Cast list (page 23)
- Speaking words (page 24)
- Make a speech (page 24)

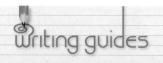

Activity 1: Thinking about issues

Objective

To improvise using a range of drama strategies and conventions to explore themes such as hopes, fears and desires.
(Year 6 Strand 4)

What to do

In this activity, the children use role play to explore issues as starting points for stories.

- With the children working in small groups provide each group with one of the scenario cards from photocopiable page 25 'Thinking about issues'. Ask each group to develop a short role play based around the issue shown on their card. Encourage them to think about the characters that are involved in their scenario, how they are feeling and how they might demonstrate their feelings (through what they say, the tone of their voice, their expressions and so on).

- Once the groups have developed their scenes, gather the class together to watch the groups take turns to perform. Can the children guess what the issue was?

- Encourage the children to begin to collect an ideas bank of issues or dilemmas. They can source them from other stories they read, from other media (newspapers or news reports on television or on the internet) and from their own experiences.

Activity 2: Trigger points

Objective

To use exploratory, hypothetical and speculative talk as a tool for clarifying ideas.
(Progression Year 6/7 Strand 1)

What's on the CD-ROM

Trigger points
- Read the trigger points and roll over the illustrations to reveal question prompts.

What to do

This lesson encourages the children to think about 'trigger' ideas and how to hook the reader's interest at the beginning of their story.

- Discuss story openings. Together read the opening paragraph from photocopiable page 10 'The Suitcase Kid'. Point out how Jacqueline Wilson announces the issue in the first sentence, then proceeds to fill in details about the characters. If there is time, read the opening paragraphs of other realistic stories and discuss what the trigger point for the plot is (a device that prompts the action of the plot).

- Open 'Trigger points' from the CD-ROM. Read the opening sentences with the children and explore what makes them effective hooks: in the first, we wonder what is inside the suitcase and what it might lead to; in the second we want to find out what went wrong when the family moved house; in the third we anticipate conflict in family relationships.

- Roll over each illustration to reveal question prompts to stimulate discussion. Then discuss some possible pathways for the stories to follow, encouraging the children to explore different ideas for each. For example, could the story be humorous or will it be hard-hitting and emotional? Make notes of the children's ideas to produce opening paragraphs. Give each child a copy of photocopiable page 26 'Trigger points' to complete independently.

 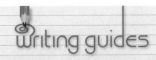

Activity 3: Storyboard

Objective

To use varied structures to shape and organise text coherently.
(Year 6 Strand 10)

What's on the CD-ROM

Media resources
- Listen to, discuss and use the 'Breaking glass' audio clip as a stimulus for plots.

What to do

In this activity, the children will develop a storyboard to map ideas for a realistic plot.

- Listen to the audio file from the CD-ROM. Discuss the type of scenario it conjures up in the children's imaginations (an accident such as a child kicking a football through a neighbour's window, glass breaking because of a house fire, or a deliberate attack by vandals). What sort of atmosphere does it create? (For example, slapstick humour, anxiety.)

- Ask the children to work in pairs to think of a scenario using the audio file as the hook. Tell them that they are going to try drawing and captioning a storyboard for their plot. Explain that a storyboard is a device that film-makers use to work out a sequence of scenes in a plot. Provide the children with copies of photocopiable page 27 'Storyboard' to map out their sequence of events.

- Bring the class back together and ask volunteer pairs to rehearse their stories orally. Invite constructive feedback, discussing which plot lines seem most fruitful and why. If some stories have moved away from reality into adventure or fantasy, remind the children that realistic stories should remain rooted in reality and use everyday happenings to explore dilemmas and feelings.

Activity 4: Subjects and scenarios

Objective

To use different narrative techniques to engage and entertain the reader.
(Year 6 Strand 9)

What's on the CD-ROM

Subjects and scenarios
- Choose a subject and scenario and type in ideas for a story based around these selections.

What to do

This lesson invites the children to choose a subject and event for the plot of a realistic story, and begin to develop ideas for a setting.

- Open 'Subjects and scenarios' from the CD-ROM. Together consider the four subjects shown and invite the children to suggest what might happen to each when linked to the four different scenarios. For example, the main character might be feeling very lonely and unhappy and the puppy comes into their life to make them happy. Alternatively, the plot could start when a letter arrives that changes a life – the main character finds out they are adopted, for example.

- As a class, choose a subject and scenario, and type in the children's ideas to answer the questions based on their selections.

- Hand out copies of photocopiable page 28 'Subjects and scenarios' and allow the children to work independently to fill in their own ideas. Invite volunteers to read their suggestions, and encourage discussion and feedback.

- Ask the children to work in small groups to think up more ideas for subjects and scenarios that could trigger stories.

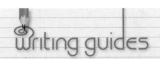

Activity 5: Scene change

Objective

To use a range of narrative devices to involve the reader.
(Progression Year 6/7 Strand 9)

What's on the CD-ROM

Media resources
- Use the 'Moving house' image as stimulus for writing.

Scene change
- Complete sentences for a story planner.

What to do

This activity invites the children to think about how setting can provide a stimulus for events that shape a plot.

- Look at the 'Moving house' photograph on the CD-ROM. Ask the children what is going on and if any of them has experienced a house move. List some of the reasons a family moves, being sensitive to individual circumstances. (A bigger house, a smaller house, a job change, divorce.) Suggest that an event like a house move can trigger the plot for a realistic story because characters face changes in their lives that they have to deal with, good or bad.

- Open 'Scene change' from the CD-ROM and, as a shared activity, work through and complete the sentences on the story planner. Encourage the children to explore different trigger points: a pet that goes missing or a clash with new neighbours, for example. Explore the change that a house move might bring: going to a new school, making new friends and so on. Ask the children how they think their character will feel and list appropriate words ('worried', 'sad', 'resentful').

- Hand out photocopiable page 29 'Scene change' and ask the children to work individually to fill them in and develop the idea for a realistic story plot based around a house move.

Activity 6: Campaigns and conflicts

Objective

To improvise using a range of drama strategies and conventions to explore themes such as hopes, fears and desires.
(Year 6 Strand 4)

What's on the CD-ROM

Media resources
- Use the 'Protest' image as a stimulus for role play.

What to do

This activity helps the children consider how conflict can provide content and plot in a realistic story.

- Look at the 'Protest' image on the CD-ROM. Ask the children to describe what is going on. Why do they think the trees might be under threat and why do they think the protestors want to protect the trees? Who would be the main parties involved? (Local people, local authority, developers.) How do they think the protestors are feeling? (Angry, determined, worried.)

- Arrange the class into small groups and tell them that they are going to plan a short scene that gets across the viewpoints of different parties. They should decide who is playing which role and think about what their main arguments would be. (For example, road builders might say that a new bypass would make village roads safer, but local people might say the road is taking away a valuable green space.)

- Give the groups time to plan and rehearse their scene then invite them to perform in front of the class. Encourage constructive feedback.

- Hand out photocopiable page 30 'Campaigns and conflicts'. Tell the children to work in pairs to fill it in. Encourage them to draw on personal or local events if they can.

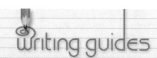

Activity 7: The lead role

Objective

To use a range of narrative devices to involve the reader.
(Progression Year 6/7 Strand 9)

What's on the CD-ROM

Media resources
- Use the images to generate ideas for main characters.

The lead role
- Type in information to describe a character.

What to do

In this activity, the children focus on creating a character to take the lead role in a story.

- Look at the images from the 'Media resources' section of the CD-ROM. For each image, think of some ideas as a class for the main character that a story might be based around (for example, the boy with the pet or the child in the family scene).

- Discuss the qualities the main character needs to have and why: we need to like them, believe in them, empathise with them and want them to succeed so that we become engaged in the plot of the story. If possible, refer to some examples of likeable, believable main characters from stories the children have read, such as Andrea in *The Suitcase Kid*.

- As a class, choose one character. Open 'The lead role' from the CD-ROM and, as a shared activity, create a character profile.

- Hand out photocopiable page 31 'The lead role' and ask the children to complete the sheet for the main character in a story idea from photocopiable page 28 'Subjects and scenarios' or photocopiable page 30 'Campaigns and conflicts'.

Activity 8: Cast list

Objective

To set their own challenges to extend achievement and experience in writing.
(Year 6 Strand 9)

What's on the CD-ROM

The Battle of Bubble and Squeak
- Text extract to read and discuss.

Media resources
- Use the 'Pets' image as a stimulus for writing.

What to do

In this activity, the children work on characterisation for the plot of an animal- or pet-centred story.

- Briefly re-read Extract 2 (on the CD-ROM or photocopiable page 11 'The Battle of Bubble and Squeak'), and recap the subject of Philippa Pearce's story: the gerbils Bubble and Squeak who are causing rows in the Sparrow family. Suggest that the dynamics for the plot come from conflict again (as with the protest-type story) as mum wants to get rid of them and Sid is desperate to keep them.

- Display the image of the pet and owner from the 'Media resources' section of the CD-ROM. Discuss, with the children, some ideas for realistic stories centred around a pet. For example, a pet gets lost or stolen, does something clever or brave or naughty and so on.

- Hand out photocopiable page 32 'Cast list' and tell the children to work in pairs to complete it. When they have finished, invite volunteers to explain their ideas for pet stories and encourage discussion and feedback.

- As an extension activity, the children could try finding out about other realistic stories which have animal or pet subjects and use the photocopiable sheet as a template to make notes about the story.

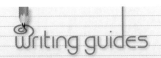

Activity 9: Speaking words

Objective

To develop drama techniques to explore in role a variety of situations and texts or respond to stimuli.
(Progression Year 6/7 Strand 4)

What's on the CD-ROM

The Suitcase Kid, The Battle of Bubble and Squeak, and The Locker Room
- Text extracts to read and discuss.
- Focus on dialogue.

What to do

This activity focuses on creating dialogue to convey conflict and characters' feelings, and using appropriate conventions of dialogue, including variation in speech words and punctuation.

- Tell the children that they are going to focus on writing dialogue. Refer back to examples of dialogue in the three extracts in Section 1. Choose a section of dialogue and model writing a few lines on the board. Point out features such as the use of punctuation for emphasis or to convey emotion (exclamation marks), use of synonyms for 'said' ('cried', 'hissed') and the informal style/incomplete sentences that can be used for speech but are not always appropriate in narrative.

- Arrange the class into pairs and give each pair one of the prompt cards from photocopiable page 33 'Speaking words'. Ask them to use the situation as the basis of a role play in the form of a conversation between the two characters.

- Choose several pairs to share their role play with the rest of the class. As the other children listen to the dialogue, ask them to make a list of synonyms for 'said' that would match the tone of the conversation ('shouted', 'yelled', 'whispered' and so on).

- Make a class list of the different 'speaking' words and ask the children to add to the list as they come across examples in their reading.

Activity 10: Make a speech

Objective

To reflect on how working in role helps to explore complex issues.
(Year 5 Strand 4)

What's on the CD-ROM

Media resources
- Use the 'Family scene' image as a stimulus for writing dialogue.

Make a speech
- Type dialogue into speech bubbles.

What to do

The aim of this activity is to encourage the children to think about viewpoints and write convincing dialogue.

- Look at the 'Family scene' image on the CD-ROM. Ask the children what they think is going on. Can they describe the situation and how they think each family member is feeling about it?

- Arrange the class into small groups and ask them to improvise a short scene using role play to convey the situation and how the family members are feeling. Allow them time to rehearse their dialogue.

- Open 'Make a speech' from the CD-ROM. Explain to the children that they are going to use the speech bubbles to script part of their dialogue showing the conflict between characters. Recap on the use of punctuation and variation in speech words (not just 'he said', 'she said') to convey emphasis and emotion.

- Ask the children to complete the activity in groups, either on screen or using photocopiable page 34 'Make a speech'.

- Invite groups to read their dialogue to the class and encourage constructive feedback.

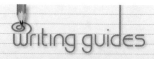

Thinking about issues

● Decide what is going on in each scene and improvise a short drama that explains the situation and how the characters feel about it.

"This is Carly," Dad said. "Your new stepmum." How I hated her.

War began with the neighbours when they cut down our tree.

I thought Gemma was my best friend, until I found out she had betrayed me.

So now I have to share a bedroom with a stepbrother I don't even know. It's not fair.

"Who said you could have a party?" Mum said. "And who is going to clear up?"

Matt is a cheat and a bully. He got me into trouble with the teacher but it wasn't my fault.

Trigger points

● Read the trigger points and for each one write an opening paragraph about what happens next.

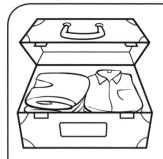

1. As soon as I opened it, I realised it was not my suitcase.

_____

_____

_____

2. It all began to go wrong the day we moved house.

_____

_____

_____

3. "This is my new girlfriend," Dad said. I looked at Tom. Neither of us said anything.

_____

_____

_____

Storyboard

- Use this storyboard to draw and caption the main sequence of events in your story. If you need to, use the other side of the sheet to add more boxes.

Subjects and scenarios

- Choose a subject.

 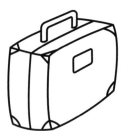  

| Puppy | Suitcase | Handwritten letter | Sports trophy |

- Choose a scenario.

| Causes trouble | Makes someone sad |
| Makes someone happy | Changes a life |

- Answer the following questions based on your selections above.

Where will your story be set?
Who is your main character?
What dilemma/issue/problem do they face?
How do they feel about it?
What happens in the end?

Illustrations © 2010, Andy Keylock/Beehive Illustration.

Scene change

● Plan your story about a house move by completing the points below.

● The trigger point for the story is _____

_____

● The main character in the story is _____

_____

● Their family is moving because _____

_____

● They are moving to _____

_____

● My main character feels _____

_____

● Their life is going to change because _____

_____

● At the end of the story they feel _____

_____

● They feel like this because _____

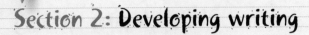
Section 2: Developing writing

Campaigns and conflicts

● Use this sheet to plan the plot for a story based on a campaign or protest.

What is the subject of the campaign or conflict in your story?
Who are the main parties involved?
What are the main arguments on each side?
How is your main character involved and what does s/he do?
What happens in the end?

The lead role

● Use this sheet to plan your ideas for the main character in your realistic story.

My main character is _____

He or she is _____ years old.

He or she lives _____

The problem my character faces is _____

_____

He or she feels _____

_____

The other main characters in my story are _____

_____

● Choose a description to fit your character and complete the sentences.

> **Brave**   **In trouble**   **Upset**   **A problem-solver**

My main character is _____ because

_____

At the end of the story, my character feels _____

_____

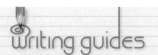

Cast list

● Use the questions to help you plan your ideas for a pet story. Use your own ideas and/or the prompts available.

1. Who is the main character in your story?

_____

2. Who or what is their pet?

_____

3. Describe the pet's character. (Use the prompts to help you.)

_____

> Brave   Funny   Clever   Naughty   _____

4. What happens to the pet in the story? (Use the prompts to help you.)

_____

> It does something clever.   It does something naughty.
>
> It causes trouble.   It gets lost.   _____

5. What is the main theme? (Use the prompts to help you.)

_____

> A rescue   A competition   A kidnap
>
> A search   _____

writing guides

Speaking words

● Decide what is going on in each scene and what you think the characters are saying.

Two friends work out how to get back at a bully.

Mum tells Ben off for letting his snake out of its glass case.

Two stepsisters argue over who gets the best bedroom.

A boy apologises because his dog has dug up the neighbour's garden.

Make a speech

● Decide what you think is going on and write some dialogue between two of the characters shown in the 'Family scene' image. Think about what each person is feeling as he or she speaks.

Character 1 _____

Speech word _____

Feeling _____

Speech word _____

Feeling _____

Speech word _____

Feeling _____

Character 2 _____

Speech word _____

Feeling _____

Speech word _____

Feeling _____

Speech word _____

Feeling _____

Section 3

Writing

Once the children have read a range of realistic stories and extracts, explored key features of the genre and completed the activities in Sections 1 and 2, they will be ready to attempt an extended piece of writing. The three writing projects in this section provide opportunities for them to develop and write an original realistic story. The timescale for completing the three writing projects can be flexible. In order to progress from initial ideas to finished stories, the children will need a number of extended writing sessions.

Practising skills

The three extended writing projects outlined in this section all provide opportunities for children to develop their speaking, listening and writing skills.

For oral work, children can discuss as a class, in small groups or with a writing partner.

For shared writing, they will learn how to use a range of simple planning frames to plan ideas for realistic stories, then turn the ideas in their shared story plans into written text using the 'My realistic story' writing templates on the CD-ROM.

For independent work, they can use the writing frames to plan and write their own realistic stories. They can present these on screen using the 'My realistic story' writing templates on the CD-ROM or on paper as a piece of extended writing.

The first project provides a starter idea for the children to develop into a plot line. The second activity provides stimuli for children to develop different plot lines for a realistic story using the planning and writing frames to support them. In the third activity, the children can choose a theme, an opening device and characters to feature in their story then use the story planner and writing templates to construct and develop the plot.

Providing support

Provide feedback and support for the children as they plan and write their own stories. Encourage them to consider how they can edit and improve their plans using prompts from the poster on photocopiable page 18 'Big issues' or by referring to the interactive version of the poster on the CD-ROM. Refer back to activities completed in previous sessions so that children can draw on their knowledge of realistic stories read in class.

Writing tips

- Write in the first or third person and past tense.
- Create a likeable main character.
- Draw on your own personal experiences where possible.
- Present your character with an issue or problem to resolve.
- Use dialogue to convey characters' feelings.
- Structure the story with an opening, dilemma or problem, then finish with a resolution.

Project 1: Story starter

What to do

This activity allows children to plan and write an original realistic story using a structured planner.

- Open 'Story starter' on the CD-ROM. Discuss possible answers to each question to generate ideas for a new story. Type in some of the children's answers to produce a simple story plan. Alternatively, children can use photocopiable page 38 'Story starter'.

- Encourage the children to produce a more detailed plan by completing the 'Story planner' on screen or on photocopiable page 43.

- Open 'My realistic story' on the CD-ROM and select a blank layout. Explain that this is going to be the first page of your story. Demonstrate how to add text and insert and resize images from the 'Image bank'. Use ideas suggested by the children to type in a simple story opening which introduces the theme and main character.

- Open a new page/template and continue writing the story. Model how to use one or two of the different templates (for example, the letter within the story and the flashback/speech or thought bubbles to record a past episode, dialogue or a character's thoughts). Involve the children, orally drafting their ideas then writing the appropriate text. When the story is complete, read and assess it with the children (in terms of content and presentation).

- Ask the children to plan, draft and write their own story about a letter that changes a character's life using the 'Story starter', 'Story planner' and 'My realistic story' writing templates.

Objective

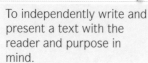

To independently write and present a text with the reader and purpose in mind.
(Progression Year 6/7 Strand 9)

What's on the CD-ROM

Story starter
- Complete a story plan.

Story planner
- Complete the story planning frame.

My realistic story
- Compose a story using the writing templates.

Project 2: Plot pathways

What to do

This activity provides stimuli for the children to develop different plot pathways using a chapter structure.

- Hand out photocopiable page 39 'Realistic plot lines'. Discuss some possible pathways to develop using each of the four themes.

- Working with a writing partner, ask the children to devise different plot lines for each theme using their own experiences where possible.

- Ask the children individually to plan a story that develops one of the plot lines. They should first use the 'Story planner' to work out the storyline either on screen or using photocopiable page 43.

- Provide the children with photocopiable page 40 'Developing character and issue'. Explain that they should use this sheet to plan out in more detail what will happen in each chapter.

- Using the ideas they have developed, the children can use the 'My realistic story' writing templates to write a realistic story following one of the plot pathways.

Objective

To use varied structures to shape and organise text coherently.
(Year 6 Strand 10)

What's on the CD-ROM

Story planner
- Complete the story planning frame.

My realistic story
- Compose a story using the writing templates.

Project 3: Choices

Objective

To experiment with different narrative form and styles to write their own stories.
(Year 5 Strand 9)

What's on the CD-ROM

Get started!
● Pick a theme and opening device for your realistic story.

Character pick and mix
● Pick two characters to feature in your story.

Story planner
● Complete the story planning frame.

My realistic story
● Compose a story using the writing templates.

What to do

This activity offers children different choices to trigger ideas for a realistic story.

● Open 'Get started!' from the CD-ROM. Click on a theme and invite children to suggest ideas for how to develop it. Next, click on an opening device and discuss how it could be used to start the themed story. You may want to use the letter idea from 'Story starter' in Project 1 to model how to begin a story using different devices, for example:

  • (Description) Darren's eyes widened as he read the letter.

  • (Dialogue) "Darren, you need to read this," Mum said. She was holding a letter.

  • (Flashback) "It had all begun in the New Year, when the letter arrived."

  • (Diary entry) 4th March. A letter arrived today. I could tell it was important from mum's face.

● Next, open 'Character pick and mix' from the CD-ROM and click to reveal two characters. Challenge the children to think how the characters might feature in the chosen theme.

● Explain to the children that they are going to plan and write a story choosing one of the themes and opening devices, and picking two characters to feature in the story. Click on more cards to explore different combinations, encouraging the children to explore the most fruitful links: for example, a false friend might feature in a story about bullying (they are secretly on the side of the bully) or a troublemaker might feature as a sibling in a story about a new step-family situation.

● Alternatively, copy and cut out a set of themes, opening devices and characters from photocopiable pages 41 and 42 and hold up each card for the children to consider and make their choices.

● Open the 'Story planner' from the CD-ROM. Complete the planner together. Type in details of the theme, opening device and characters that the children have chosen. Ask them to discuss ideas for the story opening, events and ending. Agree a suitable title for the story.

● Allow the children individually to select a theme, opening device and characters. Then provide them with time to plan and write their own realistic story, using the 'Story planner' and 'My realistic story' writing templates.

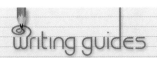

Story starter

● Imagine a letter arrives in the post that means big changes for your character. Build on this idea by answering the questions below.

1. Who is the letter from? _____

2. What does it say? _____

_____

_____

3. How will it affect your main character? _____

_____

_____

4. How does he or she feel about it? _____

_____

_____

5. What does he or she do? _____

_____

_____

6. How are things resolved in the end? _____

_____

_____

Illustration © 2010, Andy Keylock/Beehive Illustration.

Realistic plot lines

● Use the trigger points to generate possible plot lines for a story.
Use your own experiences to generate ideas where you can.

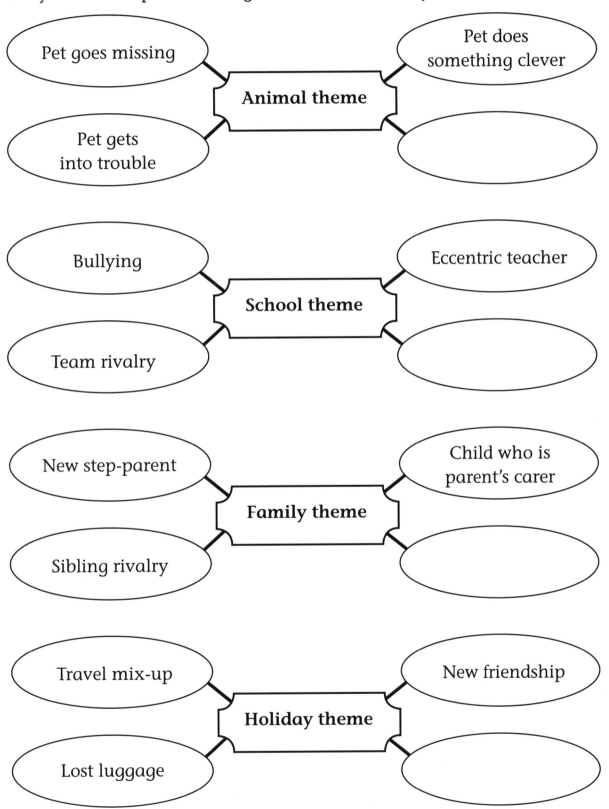

Developing character and issue

● In the first column, choose adjectives from the 'Word bank' that describe how your main character feels in each chapter of your story. Is there anything you can add that will improve your writing about how the character is feeling?

● In the second column, make notes about how the issue is developed in each chapter. Could you add anything to make the issue clearer for the reader?

	Character	Issue
Chapter 1		
Chapter 2		
Chapter 3		
Chapter 4		

Word bank

distressed

uneasy

relieved

content

relaxed

nervous

edgy

angry

exasperated

uncertain

miserable

confused

Illustration © 2010, Andy Keylock/Beehive Illustration.

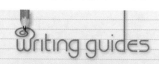

Get started!

- Cut out the cards and choose one theme and one opening device to feature in your story.

Theme	A local campaign	A family feud	Bullying	A new step-family
Opening device	Description	Dialogue	Flashback	Diary entry

SAVE OUR VILLAGE

Illustrations © 2010, Andy Keylock/Beehive Illustration.

Character pick and mix

- Cut out the cards and choose two characters to feature in your story.

A helpful adult	An animal companion	A troublemaker	A false friend
A family member	An unexpected ally	A funny character	A troubled character

Story planner

● Use the prompts below to help you plan your realistic story.

● The theme of my story is _____

_____

● The story begins with _____

_____

_____

● My main character is _____

● He or she is helped or hindered by _____

_____

_____

● The story takes place in _____

_____

● The problem or issue my character faces is _____

_____

● At the end of the story _____

_____

_____

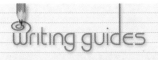

Review

This section helps the children to identify strengths and weaknesses in their own writing and to evaluate realistic stories as they read. It provides you with an opportunity to review the children's progress in achieving specific learning targets and to assess their overall attainment at the end of the unit against national standards. In assessing the children's realistic writing, it may be necessary to counterbalance a tendency to take stories into the realms of adventure or fantasy. The children should understand that when writing in this genre, characters, setting and plot all need to stay rooted in the familiar and everyday. Encourage them to keep a diary to record personal experiences they can draw on as a resource. Writing notes or taking photographs of places that could provide interesting backdrops can help to provide detail to bring story settings alive.

Self review

Involve children as much as possible in the assessment process. Photocopiable page 45 'Self review' is a self-assessment tool that the children can use independently to review how successful they have been in using some of the characteristic style or language features of the realistic genre in their own writing. You may wish to model the self-review process first, using one of the shared stories created by the class.

Peer review

Photocopiable page 46 'Peer review' encourages the use of writing partners to help children review and edit their written work. Organise the children to work with a partner of similar ability. Tell them to read then review their partner's realistic story by answering the questions and provide opportunities for feedback. Ask the children to tell their partner what they liked about their story and suggest how it can be improved. Remind them that their comments should always be constructive and supportive.

Teacher review

Photocopiable page 47 'Teacher review' has been designed to enable you to assess children's progress and attainment in writing at the end of a unit of work on realistic stories. It is linked to the eight Assessment Focuses for writing. When reviewing children's work, it is important to include observation of speaking and listening skills as well as assessment of written work. Carrying out a review will enable you to evaluate the progress that children have made towards achieving specific learning goals. Your findings can be used to set individual and group learning targets and to ensure that the next steps in learning for all children are planned at the appropriate level. The review may also highlight gaps, which can be addressed by revisiting relevant lessons in earlier sections.

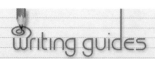

Self review

● Use this chart to review key features of your realistic story and make suggestions for improvements.

Question	Comment	How it could be improved
What is my theme or issue?		
How does the story begin (dialogue, description, flashback)?		
What makes my main character realistic and likeable?		
Is the setting realistic?		
Does the dialogue help to reveal plot and character?		
Does my main character face problems or issues?		
Does the story have a clear structure with beginning, middle and end?		
Is the issue or problem resolved in the end?		

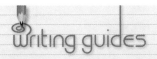

Peer review

● Answer the questions to review your partner's realistic story.

Story title: _____

Written by: _____

Question	Comment
Did the opening make me want to read on and if so why?	
What was the main theme or issue in the story?	
How realistic and likeable is the main character? Explain your answer.	
Choose a word to describe the main character and explain why you have chosen it.	
What did you like best about the story?	
Describe one way of improving the story.	

Teacher review

	AF5 Vary sentences for clarity, purpose and effect.	AF6 Write with technical accuracy of syntax and punctuation in phrases, clauses and sentences.	AF3 Organise and present whole texts effectively, sequencing and structuring information, ideas and events.	AF4 Construct paragraphs and use cohesion within and between paragraphs.	AF1 Write imaginative, interesting and thoughtful texts.	AF2 Produce texts that are appropriate to task, reader and purpose.	AF7 Select appropriate and effective vocabulary.
LEVEL 3	Some complex sentences using subordinating connectives, *e.g. if, because.* Some limited variation in tense and verb forms.	Punctuation to demarcate sentences usually accurate. Some use of speech punctuation. Commas used to divide clauses in narrative.	Openings and closings usually signalled. Attempt to sequence narrative logically.	Some links between sentences within paragraphs *e.g. using pronouns.*	Ideas and content appropriate to realistic genre included. Attempt to adopt narrative viewpoint.	Some attempts at style appropriate to realistic genre, with attention to reader.	Simple vocabulary, generally appropriate for realistic genre used. Some words selected for effect or occasion, *e.g. punchy dialogue.*
LEVEL 4	Some variety in length, structure or subject of sentences. Use of some subordinating connectives, *e.g. if, when, because.* Some variation in tense and verb forms (*e.g. past tense, participles*).	Sentences demarcated accurately throughout the text. Speech marks to denote speech with some other speech punctuation (*e.g. question marks, exclamation marks*). Commas used to mark clauses.	Narrative organised by time sequence.	Paragraphs help to organise narrative content.	Ideas and content relevant to realistic story chosen. Narrative viewpoint established and maintained.	Main features of realistic form are clear and appropriate. Style generally appropriate to realistic genre.	Some evidence of deliberate vocabulary choices *e.g. synonyms for 'said'.*

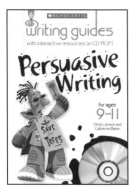

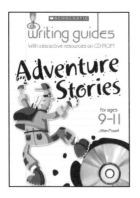